Sails in the Wind

Sails in the Wind

Hans Jürgen Hansen

Foreword by Alan H. Paul, OBE

A Studio Book

The Viking Press · New York

Segel voll Wind
© 1973 Gerhard Stalling AG, Oldenburg
and Hamburg

Published in England under the title of
Wind in the Sails

English language translation and
Foreword
Copyright © 1974 by Ian Allan Ltd.

Published in 1974 by The Viking Press, Inc.,
625 Madison Avenue, New York,
N.Y. 10022

Published in Canada by The Macmillan
Company of Canada Limited

SBN 670-61531-5

Library of Congress catalog card
number: 73-20663

Photographs by
Horst Baumann, Helmut Beckmann,
Beken of Cowes, H. Betzler, Peter
Cornelius, Martin Frank, Wolfgang Peter
Geller, Henni Goes, Zygmunt Grabo-
wiecki, Theo Kampa, Rudolf Koppen-
hagen, Siegfried Lauterwasser, Evelinde
Manon, Hermann Nafzger, Wolfhard
Scheer, Horst Schlichting, Sven Simon,
Roger M. Smith, Jörn Storch, Franz
Thorbecke and Benno Wundshammer,
as well as from the photo archives of
Bavaria-Verlag, Stern, Süddeutscher
Verlag, Yacht Photo Service, and
Yachting World.

Printed in Germany

FOREWORD

This book of photographs captures and holds superbly the many and varied facets of sailing; the beauty and colour of sails and the sea, the tranquility of leisurely cruising and the excitement of a fiercely contested race.

First, a picture of Cowes Week regatta where a mixed bag of small craft are starting on the second round of the course, with the Royal Yacht Squadron Castle in the background. Nowadays Cowes Week in Admiral's Cup years is the greatest of all regattas. The small classes are declining and are vastly outnumbered by a great fleet of cruisers racing on time allowance. In 1973 over 130 large ocean racers were entered in Class I for the handicap races, apart from other classes, and 16 nations were competing for the Admiral's Cup. On the Wednesday, wind and tide conspired to bring in all classes together to the finish with the big ocean racers at full stretch trying to get through a hoard of little boats to save precious seconds over the line. It was drama of the highest order.

In the course of over forty years of cruising, racing and organising ocean races I have been fortunate in visiting many of the great regattas at which these pictures were taken. Sometimes they were centenary celebrations of major yacht clubs and these were most spectacular occasions; Cowes, Kiel, Heligoland, Copenhagen, Hankö Morstrand, Sandhaven, Helsinki— each had its own flavour and national personality. These regattas were meetings of old friends engaged in great rivalry afloat and conviviality ashore; they found new friends, tried new drinks and explored unknown territory and novel entertainment.

Most of the Olympic Classes too are shown on these pages, from the single-handed Jolle boat of 1928 to those in the Games of 1972. It might be said, however, that the Olympics have given more encouragement to gadgetry and skill than to progress in design. Several of the classes were elderly when adopted and yet have maintained their places for many years.

There has been an explosion of dinghy classes in the last decade and thousands of young people have become expert in racing, rules, tactics, sail trimming and helmsmanship. If they wish to graduate to what I think is the greater satisfaction of cruising and racing in bigger yachts, they start with a great advantage.

Among the many interesting photographs of cruising vessels from the Baltic to Santorini one finds a Thames barge, also the new version of the old *America* and several yachts based on the traditional fishing and trading types from the coastal waters of Holland and Germany.

To my mind, the ocean racers remain the most exciting of the big yachts. In this field, developments have been phenomenal and international competition such that it seems necessary to many owners to build a new and, hopefully, a better boat every two years. Fortunately, in spite of rating rules, few designers can bring themselves to produce ugly boats. It is a lovely sight to see a large fleet set off with spinnakers of many colours and patterns (though some may think it overdone in the ketch on page 77 with the main and mizzen and spinnaker, staysail and mizzen staysail all in horizontal stripes of yellow, two shades of red, black, white, blue and green.) However, photographers must give thanks, because it is far more difficult to compose a striking picture in black and white than in colour.

It has been a great joy to go through these pages and to relive so many happy memories of excitement and comradeship and the beauty of yachts under sail.

Royal Ocean Racing Club, A. H. P.
St. James's Place, London.

Sailing was one of man's initial discoveries in the harnessing of the forces of nature to his own use. Watercraft—dugout canoes and rafts—were among the first means of travel to be discovered, and sometime in prehistory a man floating on a raft with the current must have noticed that he progressed more quickly with the wind at his back. He had then perhaps erected odd branches and pieces of bush in order to catch the wind's strength, whereupon finding that he could, as we would say today, 'sail before the wind', he became the first sailor. Indeed, the joy of feeling his craft driven forward by the wind must have been very similar to that of the modern youngster who for the first time in his life hoists sail on a tiny craft.

Later generations made use of windproof bass, straw or rush mats, instead of the leafy branches and finally, webs of cloth were woven and sewn together to make sails. The early Egyptians had knowledge of sails and yards and of many of the shipbuilding materials that remain with us today. The Phoenecians, Greeks and Romans, Chinese, Arabs and Polynesians, Vikings, Venetians, Hanseatics, Spanish, Dutch and English, developed the art of shipbuilding over thousands of years. The construction of hulls, the evolution of rigging, sails and sailing techniques progressed steadily towards perfection. Thus, at the beginning of the nineteenth century, before the arrival of the steamship, all traffic between continents was carried out by sailing ships. Even for the rest of that century these great trading ships continued to dominate the seas, they reached their peak in the Clippers and the giant steel-hulled sailing ships like the full rigged ships 'Preussen', 'Cutty Sark' and 'Thermopylae'.

These great sailing ships were steadily supplanted on the oceans by steamships and, finally, by motorships. But even as this happened, there was a remarkable upsurge in the popularity of sailing and yachting as a sport. The sport itself had traditional roots dating back to the pleasure yachts of seventeenth century kings and princes, in

sailing contests between fishermen, in pilot cutters plying for trade and even among the pirates who competed for the booty of a heavily laden East Indian.

Private sailing was however for a long time the sport of princes. One of the first contests between two yachts built purely for sport was won in the seventeeth century in England by the Duke of York from his brother King Charles II on the Thames. Most of the oldest and most famous European yacht clubs were founded either by kings or under active patronage. In 1820 the Royal Yacht Club (later, Squadron) was formed in England. Similar clubs under royal patronage were later formed in Sweden, Russia, Denmark, Belgium, Holland, Norway, Spain, Italy and Greece. Likewise, Kaiser Wilhelm II of Prussia was commodore of the Royal Yacht Club in Kiel (now known as the Kiel Yacht Club).

Since then conditions have changed greatly and sailing is no longer a privileged sport. This is only too evident on weekends when rivers, lakes and seas are crowded with fleets of holiday sailors. Millions find sailing to be the greatest sport in the world, the fulfillment of a yearning for freedom, an escape from the mechanization and the bustle of the twentieth century world.

Above: Fleets of sailing boats of all sizes in front of the "Castle", the old clubhouse of the Royal Yacht Squadron in Cowes on the Isle of Wight, where once Edward VII and his nephew Kaiser Wilhelm II competed.

Now fleets of sailing boats of all sizes make up a scene which could be Kiel Bight (pictured overleaf) or Long Island Sound or one of countless other stretches all over the world on any summer's day.

Previous page: 5.5 metres with spinnakers running before the wind on Urner Lake, Switzerland.

Right: Finns from Holland, Switzerland, Austria, and West Germany at the start of a regatta at Kiel.

The tiniest boats now sailed are smaller than 10 ft (3 m), the largest (with the exception of the few dozen large sailing ships sailing as training ships) measure about 70 ft (20 m) long. Boats differ mainly in that some have drop keels (such as open racing and day boats and cabin cruisers) while others are keelboats. The drop keel, which hangs in its watertight compartment amidships, can be drawn up and the drop keelboat can therefore be used in shallow water. It can however capsize but is usually made unsinkable by the use of flotation bags and thanks. In contrast, the keelboat has a fixed ballast keel, this sets the centre of gravity of the boat so deep that whatever the angle of roll it will always right itself. One variety of the drop keel boat is the centre board yacht. There are also the multihull boats (catamarans and trimarans) and boats with bilge keels. The Dutch are very fond of the latter which they developed from boats which sailed on the Zuider Zee, or converted from flat-bottomed hulls.

Before World War I, rules had already begun to be laid down for the construction of racing yachts. The International Yacht Racing Union *(IYRU)* in which all countries interested in racing are represented, concerns itself with international class specifications and handicap formulas for offshore racing. For the individual classes, maximum and minimum measurements for the main hull dimensions and for sail area are laid down. Inside these tolerances, each class is allowed some variation in design and construction. For offshore racing, ratings or handicaps are worked out. The endeavour here is to discriminate mathematically between the effects of different displacements, hull shapes and characteristics, between materials and forms of construction, as well as the differences rigs and areas of sail have on the speed of yacht, and they express the result as a time correction factor *(TCF)*. The elapsed sailing time is then multiplied by the *TCF* to yield the corrected time upon which race results are decided. The International classes of standard boats may only be built according to the very precise IYRU specifications. At the present time six of the International classes are also Olympic classes, although selection changes from time to time. All boats of the International classes carry their country letter next to their class insignia and their individual number. For example, the letter for the United Kingdom is 'K', for West Germany it is 'G', East Germany, Austria and the United States have the double letters 'GO', 'OE' and 'US' respectively, the letter for Holland is 'H' and for Switzerland 'Z'. Besides the International classes, each country has developed national and local classes to meet specific sailing conditions. For these classes individual insignia and sail numbers are carried. Yacht classes for the most part are developed from a specific designer or builder, the popularity of certain mass produced types eventually making them suitable to sail as a class. A class organisation is set up and in due course it becomes recognised by the central sailing authorities and regatta organisers. The so-called *'Metre boats'* have been well known since early in the century. *'Metre'* means that under a measurement formula they are rated at a specific length—namely *12 metre, 10 metre, 8 metre* and *6 metre* for racing purposes. Among the *Metre boats* still in use are the *12 metre* yachts, which have again become popular and since 1958 have been used in the America's Cup Races. The *8 metre* yacht was an Olympic class from 1900 to 1936, as was the 5-man crewed *6 metre* which had 540 sq ft of sail. However the latter was superseded in the 1952 Olympics by the 3-man crewed *5.5 metre* yachts with about 330 sq ft of sail area. The 5.5's remained Olympic boats until 1968. At the 1972 Olympics, the classes *Finn, Flying Dutchman, Star, Tempest, Dragon* and *Soling* took part. At the 1976 Olympics the *Stars* and *Dragons* will be replaced by *International 470's* and *Tornado* Class catamarans.

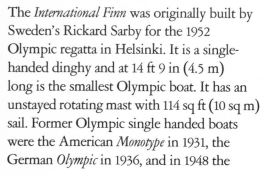

The *International Finn* was originally built by Sweden's Rickard Sarby for the 1952 Olympic regatta in Helsinki. It is a single-handed dinghy and at 14 ft 9 in (4.5 m) long is the smallest Olympic boat. It has an unstayed rotating mast with 114 sq ft (10 sq m) sail. Former Olympic single handed boats were the American *Monotype* in 1931, the German *Olympic* in 1936, and in 1948 the British *Firefly*. The picture above shows a Dutch *Finn* off the North Sea coast; the one below, German *Finns* at a turning mark during Kiel Week.

The *International Flying Dutchman* (1951) designed by the Dutchman Uffa van Essen, has belonged to the Olympic class since the Naples Olympics in 1960. It is a very lightly built two-man crewed dinghy, for which the *IYRU* allowed the use of a trapeze for the first time. This device is a line made fast to the top of the mast, on which the crew, suspended from a belt, can lean out horizontally, thus ensuring that the boat sails as upright as possible allowing the optimum sail trim for sailing to windward, as shown in the above picture.

Left: *Flying Dutchmen* broad reaching with their spinnakers up.

Two views of *Flying Dutchmen* racing.

Above: Against the backdrop of the mountains on Lake Constance, Switzerland, half-filled spinnakers with wind dead astern.

Right: On the Zuider Zee, getting the most out of the wind by making maximum use of the trapeze.

Two classes of two-man keelboats taking part in the 1972 Olympic regatta: the *Star,* a participant since 1932, taking part for the last time, and a *Tempest* competing for the first. The trapeze fitted *Tempest* was designed in glass reinforced plastic (GRP) by Jan Proctor. To a certain degree this is a dinghy, having a fixed keel instead of a drop keel. Its length is 22 ft (6.70 m) and its sail area 247 sq ft (23 sq m). Right: A British and a Norwegian *Tempest* at a turning mark. Below: A fleet of *Tempests* reaching with spinnakers.

The *Star,* designed by the American Francis Sweisguth in 1911, was for decades one of the world's most popular racing boats. Originally built of wood, and now made of synthetic material, the *Star* is 22 ft 7½ in (6.92 m) long and has a 285 sq ft (26 sq m) sail area. *Stars* carry a red star as class insignia. Star sailors founded the oldest existing racing class association—the International *Star* Class Yacht Racing Association in New York. Above: *Stars* in a strong wind make for the finishing line after rounding the mark. Left: A group of *Stars* running before the wind.

Above: *Stars* with wind abeam. Left: A
British *Soling* surfing over the swell with a
Flying Dutchman in the background.
Following double page: *Solings* with well-
filled spinnakers running before the wind.

The *Soling* has been an Olympic boat since
1972. Designed by the Norwegian Jan Linge
this 27 ft (8.15 m) three-man keelboat
of synthetic material has a 233 sq ft
(21.7 sq m) sail area.

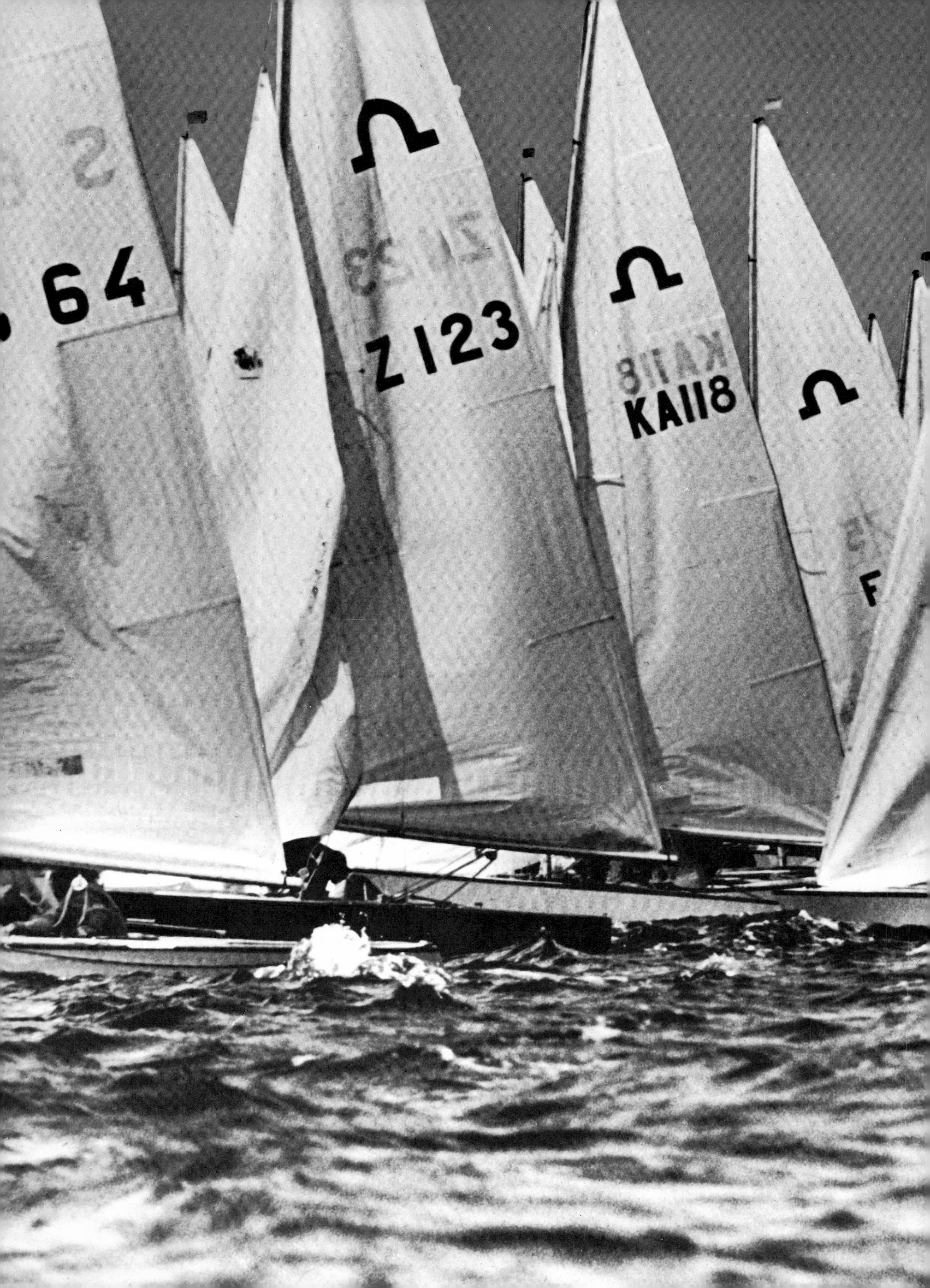
64
Z123
KA118

Preceding double page: *Solings* from France, West Germany, Denmark, Switzerland and Australia crowd in on a mark in a slack wind. The *Dragon,* a wooden boat just under 30 ft (8.90 m) long and with a 267 sq ft (22 sq m) sail area, was designed by the Norwegian Johan Anker in 1929. It was the foreunner of the *Soling* as the Olympic three-man keelboat from 1948. The first of the *IYRU* recognised standard keelboats to have a cabin, the *Dragon* developed into an outstanding racing boat and the modern version owes little to the original design. This seaworthy craft is particularly favoured in the Baltic, North Sea and English Channel.

Above left: *Dragons* round the marker buoy
during a race. Right: *Dragons* passing the
East Gurnard buoy in the roadstead at
Cowes. Following double page: Two *Dragons,*
one French the other Swiss, in a freshening
breeze in the light of the evening sun.

It is impossible to overlook the vast numbers of dinghies and smaller keelboats, beginning with what is probably the most popular small one-man dinghy in the world, the American *Optimist*. A dinghy only 8 ft (2.30 m) long with a quadrilateral 35 sq ft (3.5 sq m) lugsail, it is a typical 'beginner's boat', with which even children can sail in regattas. Popular one-man dinghies are also those of the *Moth* class of 11 ft (3.35 m) length and 82 sq ft (7 sq m) sail area, much sailed by the English, French and Belgians, and the *OK* dinghy designed by the Danish boat builders Knud and Axel Olsen, an excellent boat for the young, 13 ft 2 in (4 m) long with 90 sq ft (8.3 sq m) of sail area. There is also the *Laser* off-the-beach-boat, designed by Bruce Kirby, and recently recognised by the *IYRU*. Among the two-man dinghies, a prime example especially designed for young people is the *International Cadet*. It measures 10 ft 7 in (3.22 m) long and has a 56 sq ft (5.65 sq m) sail area. Another in this class is the *Flying Dutchman*, designed by Uffa van Essen, who also developed the *Flying Junior*. There is also the German *Pirat* dinghy hard-chined, (16 ft 6 in [5 m] long with a 108 sq ft [10 sq m] sail area), which was designed in 1938 by Carl Martens. During World War II, the so-called 'People's Boat' *(Folkboat)* was developed in Sweden. Of robust and seaworthy clinker built construction, the *Folkboat* was especially designed for the less well-to-do sailor and today remains a

much-loved racing and cruising boat all over Europe. Its length is 25 ft (7.64 m) and it has a 258 sq ft (24 sq m) sail area. Variations of these Nordic *Folkboats* have taken part in Atlantic races. The photograph above left shows *Folkboats* during a regatta in the Wendemarke, and the one at centre shows similar boats from windward in a close fetch. Another *Folkboat* (below right) is seen trimming to the wind with a little assistance from its moveable ballast. The photograph below is of an *Olympic* dinghy and the one above, at far right, shows British *Mirror* dinghies, one of the most rapidly growing classes in the UK. Jack Holt and Barry Bucknall were responsible for the design of this dinghy of which about 30.000 have already been made.

Above left and right: A Dutch one-man dinghy of the *International Contender* class sailing with the trapeze in a stiff wind. This small craft has a single partly battened sail on a bendy mast and handling it calls for agility, fitness and real sailing skill. In the photograph below left the crew of an *International 470* dinghy hangs onto the trapeze with wind broad on the beam and the spinnaker set shy. In 1976 these two-man sailing boats are to be accepted as an Olympic international class. They have a length of 4.70 m (15 ft 6 in), hence the name, and a sail area of 137 sq ft (12.7 sq m). Other international two-man dinghies are those developed by Britain's John Westell in 1953 and called the *International 5-0-5* from their length of 5.05 m (16 ft 6 in) which, with 172 sq ft (16.3 sq m) of sail area can be sailed with a trapeze. There is also the *International Snipe* of 15 ft 6 in (4.72 m) length and 128 sq ft (10.7 sq m) sail area designed by the American William Crosby in 1931; the *International Vaurien* of 13 ft 3 in (4.08 m) length and 88 sq ft (8.8 sq m) sail area, designed by the Frenchman Jean-Jacques Herbulot; the *International Sharpie* designed by H. Kroger in 1927, whose last race as an Olympic boat was in Melbourne in 1956, and the immortal *International 14 ft* dinghy which was first given international status in 1928 and has continually developed since. There are large fleets still racing in Britain, the United States and Canada.

Of the numerous examples of national class two-man dinghies, among the best known in Europe are the French *Zef,* only 12 ft (3.67 m) long and carrying 91 sq ft (8.5 sq m) of sail, a good training boat; the Dutch *Schakel,* 15 ft 3 in (4.20 m) long; the *420 dinghy,* designed by Christian Maury of the Royal Netherlands Yachting Union, which has 110 sq ft (10.25 sq m) of sail area; the Italian *Strale,* built by Santarelli on Lake Garda, which is 16 ft 1 in (4.90 m) in length and has a 145 sq ft (12.75 sq m) sail area.

There are also the Italian *S-dinghy,* designed by V. Lombardi, which is 14 ft 11 in (4.70 m) long with a 133 sq ft (12.4 sq m) sail area; the German-built *Korsar* with trapeze and spinnaker, designed by Ernst Lehfeld, and measuring 16 ft 5 in (5 m) long with 120 sq ft (11.5 sq m) of sail area; the French *Ponant* designed by Descamps (17 ft 3 in [5.25 m] long with a 175 sq ft [16 sq m] sail area); the US *Lightning,* designed by the celebrated American offshore designers, Sparkman and Stephens, and measuring 19 ft (5.79 m) long

with a 177 sq ft (16.50 sq m) sail area; and the British *Fireball,* designed by Peter Milne, which is 16 ft 2 in (4.95 m) long, has a 123 sq ft (11.43 sq m) sail area, and belongs to an international class.

Above right and left: Boats of the Dutch *Rainbow* class (featuring a mainsail with a gaff). Below right: A two-man Danish *Trapez* dinghy, designed by Paul Elvstrom.

Above left: The *Fireball.*
Below left: A Dutch national two-man dinghy, *Schakel,* comes on to the plane revealing its hard-chine section and V-bottom. The lines of the *Lightning,* an International class boat with a three-man racing crew, and its high aspect ratio sail plan belie the craft's pre-war origin. Around 12,000 of this American boat have been built. Among the largest cabinless boats are the German *Trias.* These three-man keel boats, first built in 1967, are 30 ft 6 in (9.20 m) long, and have a 308 sq ft (28.7 sq m) sail area. Another boat in this category is the British *Daring* which measures 33 ft (10.06 m) long and has a 311 sq ft (29 sq m) sail area.

Above right: a *Daring* sailing hard into the wind.

In contrast to the open dinghies and keel-boats, the cabined boats are often racing boats also. They have, as their name indicates,

closed cabins for casual or long term use. Among these are the more comfortable family cruising and weekend sailing boats, types built for vacations, which are raced less frequently than those specially developed or converted for racing purposes and 'rated' accordingly. An example is the Finnish *Hai,* a cabin boat developed from the 1934 French national three-man *Requin* class. It has a 31 ft 6 in (9.60 m) long wooden hull, a 270 sq ft (25 sq m) sail area and three berths. For coastal waters reliable and seaworthy boats around 22 feet in length are often called 'estuary cruisers' or day boats.

Size, however is not necessarily a criterion of seagoing ability and many ocean racing craft are less than 26 feet long.

Below right: an English yacht of the 'Half-ton' class in heavy sea.

Right: a keelboat of the *Pampas* class.

No one really knows how old yacht racing is. Although there are records of the Olympic Games held on land at the time of the Greek and Roman civilizations, there is no evidence that sailing races were ever held— this is rather surprising in view of the fact that the Greeks were a seafaring people. The first known regatta as such took place in the year 1315 on the Grand Canal in Venice. During that year the first gondola race was held and this now world-famous event, takes place every year. Gondolas are not sailing vessels, however, and the first known sailing races to be organised between yachts specially built for the purpose did not occur until three hundred and more years later when Charles II arranged for such events along the Thames.

During the 19th century many more yachts were built specially for racing. Mutual encouragement, exchange of ideas and advice between racing sailors, designers and yacht builders became essential in the production of successful craft. The same holds true today with full utilization of the latest in materials and techniques which modern science has devised. An important part is also played by the major sailing associations which concentrate ideas and expertise into the improvement of a particular class of yacht. The major international dinghy classes have already been discussed. For the bigger craft, the British Royal Ocean Racing Club and the Cruising Club of America have—over the last fifty years—exercised an immense influence upon the design and performance of offshore yachts. The control of racing in the organisational sense, the establishment of acceptable international rules and conditions for races both inshore and offshore has also been the subject of continuous development since the casual early days of the sport. In this, the decisive role throughout the world has been played by the *IYRU,* and their supervision of the International Offshore Rule (IOR) has given them the influence over design formerly held by the *CCA* and *RORC.*

The majority of regattas are held for individual types or classes of boats, as their standard size and construction permits them to compete on level terms—the first boat home is the winner. In contrast, the formula classes, which are boats of differing construction and size, principally cruising boats, require some form of handicap system to even out the differences that exist between them. Inshore yacht races usually take place over triangular courses, with the first of the three legs being into the wind. The end of each leg is marked by a buoy and the starting line, which is often also the finishing line, runs between a particular mark on the shore— often a signal mast, or on the start boat—and the starting buoy. In the photograph at right boats are seen lying in thick mist around the start boat, in the background, waiting for the visibility to improve. In the foreground is the successful Italian *Star Merope II.*

A favourite regatta start is the flying start. The boats taking part can move freely until the starting gun when they must not be on the course side of the starting line. Boats over the line too soon must go back and cross it again. On the other hand, a well-timed start, together with a good windward starting position, can bring great advantages.

Above left: *Flying Dutchmen* before the start of a race. Below left: A fleet of *Pirats*. Above: Boats on a German lake.

Photographs of racing incidents are shown
on the two previous pages and here. At the
top of page 38 dinghy crews jostle for places
at a mark – a moment for cool nerves and
shrewd judgement. The second photograph
on page 38 is an aerial view of *Dragons* rounding a marker buoy on to the windward leg.
Note how the fleet has spread out rapidly
to leeward. The aerial view at the top of
page 39 shows offshore racers running under
spinnakers in a light breeze. A variety of
spinnaker staysails is to be seen. In the
picture below it, racing *Solings* are clearing
their wind after rounding a mark. Photographs such as these show what a wet
business yacht racing can be.

On this page, above left: a *Soling* goes about.
Above right: Changing sail on an ocean
racing yacht. Left and right: Two pictures of
Finns. The photograph at bottom and those
on page 41 illustrate how by lying well out-
board, the skipper, with his feet well secured
and the extreme position of the foredeckhand
on the trapeze, succeeds in counteracting the
effects of a buffeting wind. The boats are,
respectively, a *Flying Dutchman* and a British
National *Hornet.*

The length of course sailed is regulated
according to the size of the various competing classes, and this can differ greatly. For

example, the official Olympic distance for *Finns* is 6 nautical miles, for *Flying Dutchman,* 10 nautical miles. The course set down by the International Committee for *Stars,* is likewise 10 nautical miles long. The individual legs of the three-cornered course follow a definite pattern and may be sailed in either direction until the required distance has been covered and the boats cross the finishing line. During races, a shortening of a course can be ordered if weather and wind require it. This is shown by the hoisting of the international signal flag 'S' on the race committee's boat. Any adjustment of the starting time or alteration of the finishing line is indicated by the same signal.

Over a race meeting or class regatta, the results achieved by the participants in a series of races are worked out in points and adjusted by one of a number of systems. The simplest is the evaluation by minimum points, in which the first boat gets one point, the second two points, and so on. The standard points system used for the Olympic games is much more complicated but the principle is the same–the boat with the lowest points is the winner. In Olympic classes seven races are sailed but the six best races only count towards the total.

In general, regattas and sailing contests are organised by particular clubs or authorities who invite other clubs to take part. The host club receives the applications, collects the entrance fees, checks the measurement certificates of the boats and finally hands out the prizes to the winners. It is not unknown for the president of a yacht club to have been pleased to take responsibility for a regatta, to

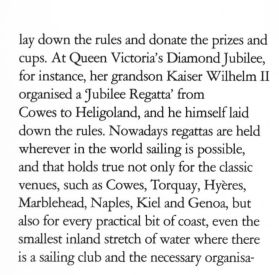

lay down the rules and donate the prizes and cups. At Queen Victoria's Diamond Jubilee, for instance, her grandson Kaiser Wilhelm II organised a 'Jubilee Regatta' from Cowes to Heligoland, and he himself laid down the rules. Nowadays regattas are held wherever in the world sailing is possible, and that holds true not only for the classic venues, such as Cowes, Torquay, Hyères, Marblehead, Naples, Kiel and Genoa, but also for every practical bit of coast, even the smallest inland stretch of water where there is a sailing club and the necessary organisa-

tion can be carried out. At the great and famous regatta weeks mentioned above, many inshore classes compete and there are also offshore races which at least in part cover long distances on the open sea. In the individual class, championship events are organised on a national, continental and world basis. Venues for those major events tend to rotate but in some classes, for example the *Stars,* it is the custom for the world championship to take place in the country of the holder.

The pictures on these and the previous four pages give some idea of how hard crews and boats have to be trained for major yacht races. Hulls must be painted and polished, rigging adjusted to a fine point of tune, sails trimmed to perfection to get the last ounce of effort out of the wind. For the helmsman, skill must be reinforced with superb physical fitness and mental alacrity if he is to endure the rigours and strains of a racing series. Even the greatest knowledge of seamanship does not, however, prevent a boat from capsizing when hit by a sudden squall, as is seen on the left. Taken during the world championships in 1972 at Solina, the skipper of a *Hornet* tries to right his boat by standing on the centre board.

Following double page: An evocation of yachts at the start of an ocean race.

That historic racing yachtsman, England's King Charles II, learned to sail during his exile in Holland and his first yacht was given to him in 1660 by the town of Amsterdam. The word yacht also comes from the Dutch 'jacht' or 'jaghtschip'. Dutch yachts of the 17th century were the ideal means of public transport, they also conveyed news from port to port. They provided those living on the coasts and inland waters of a land rich in water with the quickest and most comfortable means of travel for business journeys, and later for holidays. From these beginnings developed the sport and the pure delight of sailing with the wind at an intoxicating speed, a pleasure which, before the invention of steam or the internal combustion engine, could not be experienced in any other way. Because nearly all the Dutch waters, the Zuider Zee, the Wadden Zee (between the Friesian Islands and the coast) and the enormous bays are sheltered and shallow, Dutch yachts, which were the forerunners of the earlier English and American yachts, were flat-bottomed. Broad-beamed, sturdy and rotund, their hulls are characteristic of boats of shallow draught usual in the whole of the North Sea, boats which, on the ebb, can dry out on an even keel.

In the 19th century, yacht construction developed away from beamy, long-keeled flat-bottomed boats into long, slender, narrow racing yachts, with deep short ballast keels. Only recently has the joy and comfort of the stable, broad-beamed older boats been rediscovered. In this century, the last of round-bodied flat-bottomed sailing craft still remaining intact, have been bought up by enthusiasts, put in order and rerigged. There is so much room in their bulging hulls that they make delightful weekend and touring boats for the whole family. They are also excellent sailing craft and, like their forerunners of more than three hundred years, quite capable of taking part in races. The most important types of Dutch flat-bottomed yachts today are the 'botters' and the 'schouwens', which have a characteristic ronded bow and stern with deep freeboards. The most usual 'round' yachts are 'tjalken', 'lemster', 'aaken' and 'bollen'.

Right: The 'botter' yacht "De Camper", in the Watten. She was built in 1914. Note the loose footed mainsail—and somebody seems to have overlooked the topping lift.

Most round and flat-bottomed Dutch yachts have the mast stepped well forward with a long boom, loose-footed mainsail and a short-curved gaff. The foresail usually has a deep overlap on the mainsail. Lateral resistance is provided by leeboards which can be raised or lowered as required. The picture above gives a clear example of this.

The lifting tackle for the board can also be seen. Besides Holland, sailing in older types of boats is very popular in many countries. Examples include the traditional cutters, built in the style of pilot and fishing boats. Some of the smaller open ones are preferred by the crews of training ships and are used for instructional purposes in yacht schools.

Above right: Another example is this twin masted lugger on the lower Elbe.
Below right: A fishing boat converted into a cruising yacht, seen in the area of the Friesian Islands, gives an idea of the difficulties of sailing between the sandbanks and the drying-out mudflats of the North Sea coast.

Strongly built, roomy fishing boats are occasionally converted into yachts. In Germany, many of the once numerous *ewer, schauner* and *schnigger,* and other kinds of small fishing and merchant craft, have been converted in this way and have all but disappeared as working craft. In the Scandinavian countries old but repairable craft are still to be found. The most sought after are the strong, highly seaworthy double-ended pilot cutters built at the turn of the century in the yards of the famous Norwegian shipbuilder and designer, Colin Archer. Similarly in England numbers of the famous Thames barge, formerly the most familiar of English coastal sailing ships, have been converted to sport and pleasure sailing.

Right: The Thames barge *Spinaway* at Ipswich, on the east coast of England. The sprit sail on the main and mizzen mast and the large three-cornered topsail on the main mast are characteristic, as they also were of the ocean sailing yachts at the turn of the century. These Thames barges are constructed with rounded bow and fairly flat bottoms, which enable them to lie up on the dried out mud flats between tides when necessary. Different in shape from the rounded *boilers* and *botters,* these barges have a poop deck and transom and their sheer line is straight compared with the deep sheer of the Dutch craft. They are also sailed with leeboards.

Above left: Two Dutch *botters* running before the wind and (above right), a parade of *skutsjes* (small *tjalks)* off a crowed foreshore.

Following pages: A *tjalk* yacht (at left) and a *lemsteraak* yacht (right).
Both make very comfortable cruising yachts, thanks to their roomy cabins, high freeboard and broad beam. They are at their best, however, in the shallow waters for which they were designed and are less happy in the heavy seas encountered in the open ocean.

Larger, older sailing ships are coming back into use, generally as training ships. At left is a gaff schooner of traditional design and construction returning to port in a light breeze manned by a crew of cadets. Note the massive chain plates. A number of replicas of famous historical sailing ships have been made, exact in every detail. An example of this is the British *Nonsuch* based on a 17th century merchantman. Above is a view of her deck during an ocean voyage. Only materials similar to those originally used are employed. There is no aluminium, wire or synthetic material aboard, only wood, hemp and canvas. The compass however is of modern design!

Before the middle of the 19th century there was little difference between the yachts used for pleasure sailing and racing and the usual run of the speedier types of work boats. Yachts which could perform like modern ones were beyond the wildest dreams of the yachtsmen of the earlier era. Even the most capable sailor would not have dared venture on the high seas in boats of 20 to 30 feet in

length. Anything less than 100 feet was regarded as small.

A century ago sailing as a sport was practised either in very small open luggers for inshore racing or on larger yachts readily recognisable in Europe as variants of local pilot cutters and fishing boats and in the United States as variants of Grand Banks schooners.

The pressure of competition, especially in America, led to the development of more advanced designs which refined and improved the traditional hull form and rig. The greatest stimulus came from the competition for the America's Cup. In 1851 a British trophy, the Hundred Guineas Cup of the Royal Yacht Squadron, was won by the American schooner *America* commissioned by the members of the New York Yacht Club specifically to race against the English. Designed by George Steers, *America* had what was then an unconventional narrow hull and a sharp clipper bow under raked masts and a schooner rig. This type of narrow, long hulled lean-bowed ocean

racing yacht was very soon copied all over the world. The requirement for challengers for the America's Cup to sail the Atlantic further stimulated offshore yacht design. Competition intensified as ocean racing in its modern form became a sport in America in 1906 with the first Bermuda Race, and in Europe in 1925 with the first Fastnet. Many designers have had a hand in the development of the offshore yacht as we know it today—Watson and Nicholson, in Europe, and Herreshoff in the United States in the early days and, more recently, the immortal John Illingworth and the Stephens brothers, Rod and Olin.

The photograph at right shows the modern Dutch ocean racer *Sangria* beating to windward with a couple of rolls down. Note the relative size of the mainsail and the genoa. Masthead rig with large overlapping headsails are characteristics of the modern yacht. (A notch tighter on the genoa halyard would do no harm!)

In the early days of yachting, when yachts were vast and belonged to those of great wealth, owners seldom captained their craft. As in horse racing, yacht owners often placed their entry in the hands of a professional. They watched a skilled crew compete for the prize. The captain was usually an experienced Merchant Navy man and the owner, when aboard at all, went along as a passenger. Sailing by 'hired hands' has long gone out of fashion. Today, ocean sailing is more the province of amateurs, owners and crews alike. The great yachts of yesteryear have also disappeared and their smaller, modern successors are marvels of modern labour-saving design.

In the photograph at left the South African yacht *Omuramba,* a Stephens designed Class II ocean racer, and the British *Yeoman XVIII* have a private joust during a race. Both have star-cut spinnakers which are designed to be carried very close to the wind—as the burgees indicate. In the background is the ketch, *Marabu.*
On the following page is the English sloop *Firedance* under full press of spinnaker and spinnaker-staysail. It is obvious from her waves that she is very close to her maximum speed. Opposite her (on page 67) is the flushing ocean racer *Windliese XI,* also under star-cut spinnaker. The narrow triangular sail set near the mast is the so called 'Tallboy'.

One of the major European offshore sailing events is the annual North Sea Week which usually takes place at Easter. The longest race is that from Heligoland round The Skaw to Kiel. The picture below shows yachts leaving the harbour at Heligoland for the start. Among these are, far left, *Windliese XI* and, centre, *Germania VI*. In the bottom picture crews of yachts lying in the harbour tend to the needs of both boats and the inner man.

One of the most famous institutions in the history of yachting is Cowes Week early in August, with tricky sailing in the fierce tides around the Isle of Wight. The picture opposite shows the former *12-metre Flica II*, now converted to ketch rig, beating to windward off the Island.

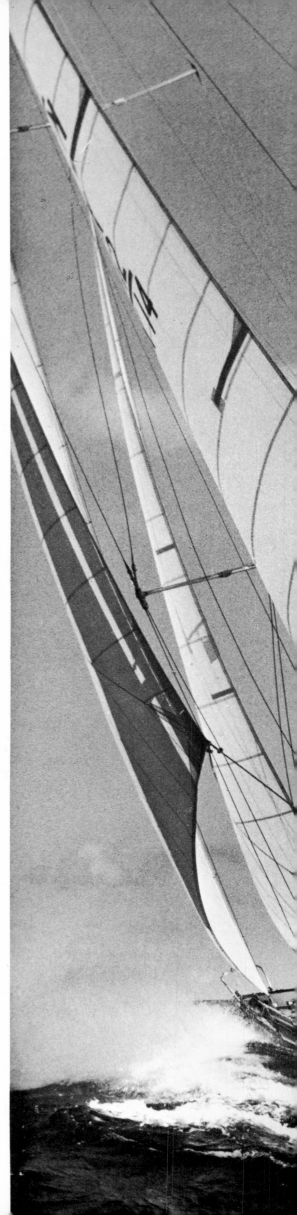

Page 70 (above): Spinnakers against the sun—*Noreyma VII, Limelight, Roundabout,* and A. N. *Other;* below, the yacht *Shinda* hurtling down wind in a race during Cowes week. On the next page, above, the sloop *Noreyma V* on a hard beat to windward off Ryde, Isle of Wight, her crew acting as moveable ballast with minimum drag; below, the sloop *Kohinoor* of the NRV prepares to set her spinnaker racing in light airs down the lower Elbe.

At the end of the last century N. G. Herreshoff, the eminent American designer, had already built a double hulled boat, based on the design of the Polynesian outrigger, but it was not until after World War II that the catamaran (with two hulls) and the trimaran (with three) attained popularity. The *IYRU* has now recognised three international classes for regattas: *Class A,* the one-man catamaran, 6 ft 6 in (2 m) maximum beam and about 150 sq ft (14 sq m) of sail area. To this type, for example, belong the 16 ft 6 in long *Shearwater III,* the 17 ft 3 in long German *Fileu* and the 19 ft long Italian *Catalina; Class B,* the two-man catamaran of 10 ft maximum beam and 230 sq ft sail area, to which the 20 ft long *Olympic Tornado* belongs; and the three-man *Class C* of 12 ft beam and 200 sq ft sail area. In addition to these are the catamarans with cabins on the platform between the hulls, including ocean racing types over 50 ft long and with a 1,000 sq ft sail area.

Double hull boats have a relatively high initial stability but they become increasingly unstable when one of the floats tilts up out of the water. With a smooth sea and a reaching wind, however, the double hull boat can achieve speeds well beyond those attainable in a single hulled yacht of similar size. The photograph at left shows a *Shearwater III* with wind abeam sailing on one hull, and the one on the right on ocean racing catamaran, running before a gentle breeze.

The deep sea sailing yacht—offshore cruisers and ocean racing yachts—have been developed quite remarkably during the last decade. The sail design, booms and rigging have been changed, so have hull shapes particularly below the waterline, the aim being to keep the wetted surface to a minimum. Gone are the deep, low aspect ratio wooden keels and keel-mounted rudders. Favored today are high aspect ratio dinghy-like fins, and bulb keels with separate stern mounted rudders, sometimes with a skeg, sometimes without.

The size of yachts regarded as suitable for racing safely in bad weather has been steadily reduced. Modern design and construction methods have produced hulls of light weight and small size but of immense strength. Similarly, masts, rigging and sails have steadily become lighter and simpler, yet stronger. The growing class of 'Quarter Ton' ocean racers are boats that are approximately 20 feet on the waterline.

Cruisers and similar classes are 'rated' for handicap—after they have been evaluated against a measurement formula, as individual boats in the same class are neither identical in size or shape nor capable of the same performance.

The 'rating' in turn is converted into a time allowance with the object of ensuring that each yacht competing in a race has a fair chance of winning. In theory, at least, given equal sailing achievements, all the yachts should each reach the finishing line at the same time. This actually happened in Cowes Week, 1973.

The general principle of the rating system is that all the speed-producing factors in a yacht's design, her length, stability and sail area shall be assessed and then adjusted to allow for other factors like beam, displacement and freeboard which may serve to slow her down.

Finally, when all the time allowances have been calculated, a further adjustment is made in calculating the race results themselves to allow for average speed over the course so that neither very small nor very large yachts benefit.

In European waters the governing rating rule was for many years that of the British Royal Ocean Racing Club—known as the 'RORC Rule'. In America the rule of the Cruising Club of America was followed, until the advent of the International Offshore Rule, which has superseded both of them. There are also national rating formulas for cruisers—racers, such as the K. R. Kreuzer-Renn formulae in Germany and in the Scandinavia the Swedish S. H. R. (Svenska Havkryssar Reglar) rule.

The two international formulas, RORC and CCA, differed essentially in the measurement of effective sailing length and in the manner of time adjustment. It was impossible simply to convert a rating under the one rule to a rating under the other without extensive remeasurement. Furthermore, since boats were specifically designed to rate well under one particular rule, in international races involving American and European yachts

certain unfair advantages existed. After years of discussion, a compromise formula was finally worked out between the RORC and the CCA rules which resulted in the International Offshore Rule (IOR). The IOR, adjusted repeatedly since it was first introduced, is now known as 'IOR Mark III'. The rating gives a measure of effective sailing length and is usually shown in feet. Yachts are then divided into class according to their rating.

In Class 1, the rating limits are from 33.0 to 70.0 ft (10.05–21.34 m); in Class 2, from 29.0 to 32.9 ft (8.84–10.02 m); in Class 3, from 25.5 to 28.9 ft (7.77 to 8.81 m); in Class 4 from 23.0 to 25.4 ft (7.01 to 7.74 m); in Class 5 from 21.0 to 22.9 ft (6.40 to 6.98 m); in Class 6 from 19.5 to 20.9 ft (5.94 to 6.37 m); in Class 7 from 17.5 to 19.4 ft (9.31 to 5.91 m); and in Class 8 from 16.0 to 17.4 ft (4.80 to 5.28 m).

But racing under a rating rule, no matter how effective the rule, is inevitably slightly artificial and recently there has been a greater demand for more 'boat-for-boat' events where all entrants raced level and first home was the winner. As a result the 'One Ton'. 'Half-ton' and 'Quarter Ton' classes were set up,'One Ton' carrying a rating of 27.5 ft (8.38 m); 'Half-ton', 21.7 ft (6.60 m) and 'Quarter Ton', 18.0 ft (5.50 m). The boats of these classes are designed or built to their particular rating and, therefore, sail against each other on equal terms.

The majority of today's ocean racing yachts are rigged as masthead sloops, yawls or ketches. The most popular type is the masthead sloop with her large foretriangle. Under IOR III, however, we may see a return to the 'three-quarters' masthead sloop and an increase in the popularity of yawls and ketches.

Above: The *Dragon*, a classic three-quarters masthead sloop sails with her spinnaker set. In contrast, is a typical masthead sloop (far left) with her large spinnaker setting high—an advantage of the rig. In the photograph near left and right are a ketch and a yawl.

Left: *Germania VI,* a yawl built of aluminium. Above: A photograph taken from *Germania VI's* main mast just as the spinnaker is about to be trimmed. The difference between a yawl and a ketch is that the rudder head in the yawl is situated before the mizzenmast, whereas in the ketch it is behind. Also, the mizzenmast is usually higher in the ketch.

Following pages: The Belgian yacht *Hermes* cruising under spinnaker down sun in an easy sea (left). Right: *Josephine VII* of the Royal Thames Yacht Club very close to be gybe; the yacht ahead has already gybed and the veteran *Cynthia,* on the port, is in the process of doing so. Pages 82–83: View on the after-deck of the 65 foot ocean racer *Sindbad VIII.*

Right: Former British Prime Minister Edward Heath's *Morning Cloud,* the second of his yachts so named. Mr. Heath is sitting alongside the helmsman.
Below: Yachts in a freshening wind.

Above: What happens when a spinnaker is carried too shy or too long in a rising wind.
Left: The yawl *Hamburg VII,* designed by the American designer, William Tripp, showing a colourful spread of spinnaker, spinnaker staysail and mizzen staysail.
Right: A yawl rigged cruiser coast crawls back to her anchorage.

The famous yacht *America* which, in 1851, took what became the 'America's Cup' to New York, was destroyed at the end of the 19th century, but the New York brewery-owner Rudolph Schaefer had a replica built according to the old lines and specifications. In the photograph below we see her sailing off the New England coast. Since 1857 there have been repeated but unsuccessful challenges to the New York Yacht Club for the America's Cup, the latest being in 1970 when the American yacht *Intrepid* was the winner. Until the early part of this century, the contest was between individual challengers and defenders without design restrictions and the United States owed her successful defence largely to the genius of Nathaniel Herreshoff. After World War I and into the thirties, the vast 'J' Class yachts, 130 feet long and with masts 160 feet high, competed. Following World War II, however, the International *12 Metre* class was chosen and challengers had to be designed according to that rule. The first post-war challenger, in 1958, was the British yacht, *Sceptre,* seen at right on sailing trials in the Firth of Clyde. She was defeated off Newport, Rhode Island by the defender, *Columbia.*

The replica of the *America* of 1851 is, perhaps, a symbol of present day nostalgia through which romantic sailing enthusiasts imagine themselves in a world entirely dependent on wind and weather, free from the world of noise, computers and industrial pollution. Not only the replica builders and the Dutch Botter and Colin Archer cutter enthusiasts belong to these romantics; the number of people seeking the freshness and exhilaration of sailing, the joys and thrills of making use of wind and water, to say nothing of the delights of nature and the surrounding scenery, is legion. Whether one wishes to go cruising in the Baltic or the Norwegian fjords with their idyllic harbours, rove the English Channel or the New England or Californian coasts, follow the routes of Odysseus along the Mediterranean's classical shores, or explore the breadth and power of the open oceans, the opportunities are plentiful. Some cross the Bay of Biscay (above) while others enjoy themselves in the sunshine off the rocky shores of Capri (right).

Too little recognised is the truth that the majority of delightful places in the world lie on the sea—the beaches, cliffs, bays, fjords and harbours. From the water—from the deck of one's boat as it approaches its destina-tion, the land shows its most beautiful face; whether it be Venice, Lisbon, Stockholm, the chalk cliffs of Dover, the bays of San Francisco, Rio de Janeiro or Hong Kong, the islands of Heligoland or Honolulu. There are

different ways of carrying out such cruises—
with one's own boat, with a chartered boat,
or as a guest, paying crew member or
partner on a chartered yacht, or else with an
owner who lacks the necessary hands for a
complete crew. In the photograph above a
ketch is sailing off the Greek islands of Santorini. On the following two pages a motor
sailer chugs, sails up, through the calm
translucent waters off the Corsican coast.

Left: 'Helm's a lee and round she goes.'
The joy of cruising under sail in the Aegean.
Above: The schooner *Colomba,* built in the
shipyard of Camper and Nicholson in 1900,
with her crew lazing in the sun on a calm
and beautiful day.
The pleasure of the world of the sailing boat

can also be enjoyed in 'small bites'. Those
short on vacation days or funds can still
spend the finest of holidays on a modest
cruising dinghy with a tent over the deck, in
a day boat or a small cabin cruiser, alone,
with a companion or with the whole family,
on inland or coastal waters. Sailing is equally

pleasurable whether or not one has a 'class'
boat or does or doesn't race. The delights of
the sport are available in a host of craft, big
and small, at a range of prices from the
custom built motor sailer to the simple
do-it-yourself kit.

Anybody who has the time, necessary financial backing, the constitution and frame of mind, and, above all, sufficient knowledge of sailing and seamanship, can venture on an Atlantic trip. The mere fact of a successful crossing will give him the greatest satisfaction. The photograph above shows the coast of Calabria in the evening sun. At right, a cruising ketch fills gently over an evening sea.

Following double page: The joy and challenge of sailing. A close reach with spinnaker shy and lee rail under.
Pages 100–101: A quiet moment during an Atlantic crossing.

Although there have been a number of transatlantic races in recent years, such competitions are not yet regular features of the ocean-racing calendar. The great classics remain the Bermuda Race held every two years from Newport, Rhode Island to Bermuda; the Trans Pac race from California to Honolulu; the races from Buenos Aires to Rio de Janeiro and from Cape Town to Rio de Janeiro, both held every three years; the tough annual event from Sidney to Hobart in Tasmania, and perhaps the greatest test of them all, the biennial Fastnet race from Cowes to the Fastnet Rock on the Irish south coast, and back to Plymouth.

The photograph below shows the cockpit of the Stephens' designed Italian yacht *Levantades* at the start of the Fastnet race. The two small flags on the backstay are Class 1 flags. At right is a photograph taken from the bowsprit of a large cruising yacht of the older type. On the following pages are the yachts *Roland von Bremen* (left), *Diana* (centre), and *Wappen von Hamburg* (right) racing at Kiel before spinnakers were fashionable. The photograph was taken by Peter Cornelius, the famous yacht photographer who was tragically killed in 1960. Pages 106–107: In the foreground, *Germania VI* sailing for Fehmarn in hazy and almost windless weather—with spinnakers very much in fashion.

After the regatta, the week-end trip or the cruise that has taken several weeks, there is still much to be done as the boat lies fast in harbour. Sails must be taken down and stowed in their bags together with sheets.

Safety belts and life belts must be put away in the ship's locker. Shrouds and other standing rigging have to be slacked off, sheets un-reeved, the main boom lashed to the boom crutch, the bilges pumped out, the deck washed down and the oilskins folded and stowed away.

Gradually, as the autumn days shorten, the last sailing day of the season approaches. Then boats are hauled up and unrigged, the bottoms cleaned and scraped of barnacles, the inside washed down and dried out. All cocks, bulkheads and doors must be opened so that the air can get in and the wood will not become damp, mildewed or rotten. Much of this work, including necessary repairs, is easier than it used to be because of today's new materials, Glassfibre boats do not rot, neither do nylon sails or ropes made of artificial fibre, even if they happen to be stored away damp. The never-ending jobs with wooden boats in early spring, scraping, sanding and painting, can now be done with handheld electric drills, sprayguns, and with hard, longlasting synthetic paints. At home one sorts through snapshots of the voyages and races made last summer, studies sailing periodicals and boat catalogues, and, bent over charts, enjoys making plans for the next season.

Right: Boats in the evening sun.
On the following page, a multi-hued spinnaker of massive proportions is dowsed—or is it a wrap?
Page 111: Sails drying in the sun flutter over boats lying in harbour.

In winter the boats lie in club sheds, on
legs on the beach, or after the drive home on
a trailer, behind or inside the garage to await
spring when once more they can go forth
on the water with their sails in the wind.